# ANTHOLOGY

# Poetry
## *Introduction 5*

# Poetry
## *Introduction 5*

FABER AND FABER
London    Boston

*First published in 1982*
*by Faber and Faber Limited*
*3 Queen Square London WC1N 3AU*
*Printed in Great Britain by*
*The Thetford Press Ltd, Thetford, Norfolk*
*All rights reserved*

*This anthology © Faber and Faber, 1982*

*British Library Cataloguing in Publication Data*
Poetry introduction
5
1. English poetry—20th century
821'.914'08 PR 1225
ISBN 0-571-11914-X
ISBN 0-571-11793-7 PBK

# CONTENTS

7

## MICHAEL HOFMANN

## MEDBH McGUCKIAN

## BLAKE MORRISON

This book has been published with financial assistance from the Arts Council of Great Britain.

# WENDY COPE

## Lonely Hearts

Can someone make my simple wish come true?
Male biker seeks female for touring fun.
Do you live in North London? Is it you?

Gay vegetarian whose friends are few,
I'm into music, Shakespeare and the sun.
Can someone make my simple wish come true?

Executive in search of something new—
Perhaps bisexual woman, arty, young.
Do you live in North London? Is it you?

Successful, straight and solvent? I am too—
Attractive Jewish lady with a son.
Can someone make my simple wish come true?

I'm Libran, inexperienced and blue—
Need slim non-smoker under twenty-one.
Do you live in North London? Is it you?

Please write (with photo) to Box 152.
Who knows where it may lead once we've begun?
Can someone make my simple wish come true?
Do you live in North London? Is it you?

## Reading Scheme

Here is Peter. Here is Jane. They like fun.
Jane has a big doll. Peter has a ball.
Look, Jane, look! Look at the dog! See him run!

Here is Mummy. She has baked a bun.
Here is the milkman. He has come to call.
Here is Peter. Here is Jane. They like fun.

Go Peter! Go Jane! Come, milkman, come!
The milkman likes Mummy. She likes them all.
Look, Jane, look! Look at the dog! See him run!

Here are the curtains. They shut out the sun.
Let us peep! On tiptoe Jane! You are small!
Here is Peter. Here is Jane. They like fun.

I hear a car, Jane. The milkman looks glum.
Here is Daddy in his car. Daddy is tall.
Look, Jane, look! Look at the dog! See him run!

Daddy looks very cross. Has he a gun?
Up milkman! Up milkman! Over the wall!
Here is Peter. Here is Jane. They like fun.
Look, Jane, look! Look at the dog! See him run!

## Score

Shadows of lamp posts
stretch across the road.

If you could pluck one
it would make a thick, deep sound.

Imagine you are travelling across the strings
of a huge grand piano.

Add to this the way leaf shadows
scrape the tarmac, softly,

and the high notes of the pavement
as it catches points of light.

Begin to hum a slow, free tune
you haven't heard before.

## On Finding an Old Photograph

Yalding, 1912. My father
in an apple orchard, sunlight
patching his stylish bags;

three women dressed in soft,
white blouses, skirts that brush the grass;
a child with curly hair.

If they were strangers
it would calm me—half-drugged
by the atmosphere—but it does more—

eases a burden
made of all his sadness
and the things I didn't give him.

There he is, happy, and I am unborn.

## At 3 a.m.

the room contains no sound
except the ticking of the clock
which has begun to panic
like an insect, trapped
in an enormous box.

Books lie open on the carpet.

Somewhere else
you're sleeping
and beside you there's a woman
who is crying quietly
so you won't wake.

## Sisters

for Marian

My sister
was the bad one—
said what she thought
and did what she liked
and didn't care

At ten she wore
a knife tucked in
her leather belt,
dreamed of *being*
a prince on a white horse.

Became a dolly bird
with dyed hair longer
than her skirts, pulling
the best of the local talent.
Mother wept and prayed.

At thirty she's divorced,
has cropped her locks
and squats in Hackney—
tells me 'God created man
then realised Her mistake.'

I'm not like her,
I'm good—but now
I'm working on it.
Fighting through
to my own brand of badness

I am glad of her
at last—her conferences,
her anger, and her boots.
We talk and smoke
and laugh at everybody—

two bad sisters.


## Advertisement


The lady takes *The Times* and *Vogue*,
Wears Dior dresses, Gucci shoes,
Puts fresh-cut flowers round her room
And lots of carrots in her stews.

A moss-green Volvo, morning walks,
And holidays in Guadeloupe;
Long winter evenings by the fire
With Proust and cream of carrot soup.

Raw carrots on a summer lawn,
Champagne, a Gioconda smile;
Glazed carrots in a silver dish
For Sunday lunch. They call it style.


## Proverbial Ballade

Fine words won't turn the icing pink;
A wild rose has no employees;
Who boils his socks will make them shrink;
Who catches cold is sure to sneeze.
Who has two legs must wash two knees;
Who breaks the egg will find the yolk;
Who locks his door will need his keys—
So say I and so say the folk.

You can't shave with a tiddlywink,
Nor make red wine from garden peas,
Nor show a blindworm how to blink,
Nor teach an old racoon Chinese.
The juiciest orange feels the squeeze;
Who spends his portion will be broke;
Who has no milk can make no cheese—
So say I and so say the folk.

He makes no blot who has no ink,
Nor gathers honey who keeps no bees.
The ship that does not float will sink;
Who'd travel far must cross the seas.

Lone wolves are seldom seen in threes;
A conker ne'er becomes an oak;
Rome wasn't built by chimpanzees—
So say I and so say the folk.

*Envoi*
Dear friends! If adages like these
Should seem banal or just a joke,
Remember fish don't grow on trees—
So say I and so say the folk.

## Christmas Triolet

for Gavin Ewart

It's Christmas, season of wild bells
And merry carols. On the floor
Are gifts in pretty paper shells.
It's Christmas, season of wild Belle's
Big party. George's stomach swells
With ale; his wife's had even more.
It's Christmas, season of wild belles,
And merry Carol's on the floor.

## Letter from a 16th Century Cottage

First thing, the leaded panes
are fogged with condensation.
You can sit here at the table,
half awake, and watch
the drops run and the clarity
of day appear, bright streams
all down the glass.

The sun casts yellow diamonds
across the ragged carpet.
We begin to move, carefully,
each one on her own pathway,
wandering outside, and back again
to shade and books, entering
and leaving worlds.

If you were here and you and I
could circle one another
quietly in these old rooms
and, slow as particles of dust
caught in a sunbeam,
learn to keep time
with their dance of silences,

our thoughts, chance happenings,
would weave themselves
into a pattern, magic,
almost frightening. You'd laugh
and bring me back to earth.
This is no place for memory
to fade—or love.

At night we light candles.
Sometimes flowers of wax
form in the flames. The heat
dissolves them but the substance
doesn't change; it finds new shapes
and cools by morning,
can't be burnt away.

## Flowering Cherries

They're street trees
And they'll bear no fruit.

When winter comes
They'll dance like witches,
Shaking off their last leaves
In a fury of despair.

But this time every year
They swell with blossom,
Move their branches carefully
And dream that they are pregnant.

## Depression

You lie, snail-like, on your stomach—
I dare not speak or touch,
Knowing too well the ways of our kind—
The retreat, the narrowing spiral.

We are both convinced it is impossible
To close the distance.
I can no more cross this room
Than Zeno's arrow.


## Thaw

Under trees
the sound is loud, irregular, staccato.

Like aged priests
more used to contemplative prayer

they are baptising us
with stiff and bony hands.


## Mr Strugnell

'This was Mr Strugnell's room,' she'll say—
And look down at the lumpy, single bed.
'He stayed here up until he went away
And kept his bicycle out in that shed.

'He had a job at Norwood library—
He was a quiet sort who liked to read—
Dick Francis mostly, and some poetry—
He liked John Betjeman very much indeed

'But not Pam Ayres or even Patience Strong—
He'd change the subject if I mentioned them,
Or say, "It's time for me to run along—
Your taste's too highbrow for me, Mrs M."

'And up he'd go and listen to that jazz.
I don't mind telling you—it was a bore:
Few things in this house have been tiresome as
The sound of his foot tapping on the floor.

'He didn't seem the type for being free
With girls, or going out and having fun.
He had a funny turn in 'sixty-three
And ran round shouting "Yippee! It's begun!"

'I don't know what he meant, but after that
He had a different look, much more relaxed.
Some nights he'd come in late, too tired to chat,
As if he had been somewhat overtaxed.

'And now he's gone. He said he found Tulse Hill
Too stimulating—wanted somewhere dull.
At last he's found a place that fits the bill—
Enjoying perfect boredom up in Hull.'


## Budgie Finds His Voice

(From *The Life and Songs of the Budgie* by Jake Strugnell)


God decided he was tired
Of his spinning toys.
They wobbled and grew still.

When the sun was lifted away
Like an orange lifted from a fruit-bowl

And darkness, blacker
Than an oil-slick
Covered everything forever

And the last ear left on earth
Lay on the beach,
Deaf as a shell

And the land froze
And the seas froze

'Who's a pretty boy then?' Budgie cried.

## The Lavatory Attendant

Slumped on a chair, his body is an S
That wants to be a minus sign.

His face is overripe Wensleydale
Going blue at the edges.

In overalls of sacerdotal white
He guards a row of fonts

With lids like eye-patches. Snapped shut '
They are castanets. All day he hears

Short-lived Niagaras, the clank
And gurgle of canescent cisterns.

When evening comes he sluices a thin tide
Across sand-coloured lino,

Turns Medusa on her head
And wipes the floor with her.

# From *Strugnell's Sonnets*

## for D. M. Thomas

### (i)

Not only marble, but the plastic toys
From cornflakes packets will outlive this rhyme:
I can't immortalise you, love—our joys
Will lie unnoticed in the vault of time.
When Mrs Thatcher has been cast in bronze
And her administration is a page
In some O-level text book, when the dons
Have analysed the story of our age,
When travel firms sell tours of outer space
And aeroplanes take off without a sound
And Tulse Hill has become a trendy place
And Upper Norwood's on the underground
Your beauty and my name will be forgotten—
My love is true but all my verse is rotten.

### (ii)

How like a sprinter you have turned and run
From me, who'd loved you almost half a year.
The world's become a fridge, there is no sun,
I hardly have the stomach for a beer.
And yet I still have my guitar to strum
And books to read and some fantastic grass
That Tony got me. I sit here and hum
The tunes we used to hear in Norwood bars—
*We are All Slobs*, The Muggers' greatest hit—
Do you remember? Once you said to me
'This is their best since *Education's Shit*',
And I agreed. But I am forty-three
And blew it when I told you I'd much rather
Listen to a jazz band, like your father.

27

Not from the stars do I my judgement pluck
Although I sometimes read my horoscope.
Today the *Standard* promises me luck
With money and with girls. One can but hope.
Astrologers may not know if you'll win
The football pools or when you'll get a screw,
But one thing's clearer than this glass of gin—
Their character analyses are true.
Cancerians are sympathetic, kind,
Intuitive, creative, sentimental,
Exceptionally shrewd and, you will find,
They make fantastic lovers, warm and gentle.
Amazing, really, that you fail to see
How very well all this applies to me.


## *Strugnell's Haiku*

### (i)

The cherry blossom
In my neighbour's garden—Oh!
It looks really nice.


### (ii)

The leaves have fallen
And the snow has fallen and
Soon my hair also . . .


### (iii)

November evening:
The moon is up, rooks settle,
The pubs are open.

# DUNCAN FORBES

## Alexander Wilson

My middle two names may make you laugh,
But I was christened to bury the dead,
I am the family cenotaph
For the younger brother my mother had.

He was the man in the photographs,
The smart lieutenant of the 12th Black Watch,
He was the ghost in the negatives
Whose uniform haunted the dressing-up box.

Somewhere in Burma, freckled, red-haired
And hot in new khaki, he died in my stead.
Monsoons were his mourners, his epitaph mud.
By the time he was my age, he was seven years dead.


## Sheltered Upbringing

Hydrangeas test the soil's acidity.
The mirror triptychs in the bedroom windows
Collect the light in narcissistic pools.
Safe in their Wellingtons and windcheaters
Peter and Jane are helping Daddy garden.
He clips the privet and they feed the bonfire.
Soon they will plant potatoes in its embers
And eat them, hard and gritty, after tea.
At dusk they listen to their bedtime story:
*Henry The Green Engine* who was immured
For disobedience like Antigone.

31

## Mother and Son

Murals of the sunset
Search the eastern wall.
On the purple carpet,
By a wad of cotton wool,
A young boy stands naked,
Spotty and irritable.

His mother goes and fetches
The bottle of calamine,
Then dabs the hot red blisters
Of chickenpox on his skin
With pink cooling blotches
On his buttocks, legs and spine.

She patiently kneels, anointing
Each pox that is driving him wild,
Almost as if she were painting
Her own 'Madonna and Child'
And the scars she was preventing
Would leave him undefiled.

## August Autumn

Ever since the news,
Your father has been obsessed
By individual trees
And the dying avenues
Which have caught Dutch elm disease.

Elms with jaundiced leaves
And stains of nicotine
Throughout the diocese
Are changing their natural green
To an August autumn brown;
And elms with no leaves at all
But rookeries scribbled among
The neat, botanically-drawn
Dead upper branches and twigs
Bring winter suddenly near.
These will have to come down
And quickly before they fall,
He says in his car beneath
With his father's walking stick
Beside the driving seat
As the only outward sign
Of the cancer in his lung
And the cancer in his spine.

At night when we go to bed,
My folded sweater prays
And my trousers genuflect
Over my bedroom chair
In attitudes of faith,
But the thoughts I try to collect
Until I drop off to sleep
Refuse to offer a prayer
To a hypothetical God.
Yet I will your father's escape
From a death of cancerous pain
And the dull uncomfortable ache
In his lower vertebrae
That wakes him or keeps him awake.
I have seen him preach to the mad
In a women's mental home,

Where he joined his hands to shape
An arrowhead on its way
To the heart of his Christian God,
And showed them how they could pray
The 'Our Father' like the sane.
But what will his God become
If the cancer attacks his brain?

As he gives you the wine or bread,
After I've watched him bless
Our son's oblivious head
Up at the altar steps
Where I have never knelt,
I read the hymnbook and wait.
But I find it nevertheless
Impossible now to forget
That your father's lifelong faith
Is an indirect result
Of an earlier painful death,
And that even Christ on the cross
In his foreign dead language screamed
A God-forsaken why
When the pain became too great.
Prayerbook and painkillers lie
On the seat of the bedside chair
By your father's side of the bed:
But oh how desolate, bare,
And unbelievably dead
Will a whole hinterland seem
To my own, I suppose, despair
When he and his certitude die.

## Requiem

With crowded mourners and surpliced priests
Sit those who were once our wedding guests,

The stern archdeacon who married us
Offers the funeral address,

And where your father read our banns
Is an empty step where his coffin stands.

The same black fleet of cars on hire
Brought him and the bridal party here

And he found it difficult not to cry
As I do, biting back tears, today

At this sad marriage of love to grief,
This funeral of a married life.

He gave you away in ritual loss:
If he were here he could comfort us.


## Sanctuary

Seagulls in a loose V formation
Fly in squadrons over the estate
Westwards on winter evenings to the Severn.
The Estuary, no doubt. Mudflats at sunset.
Buffeted by winds the seagulls rally.
Caught by the rain they hold their courses firm.

Tinted by sunlight they move comfortably,
And every evening I look up to them
As flypasts for the men returning home.

## The Field

A pasture without cows, an urban field,
A paddock grazing no gymkhana ponies.
A hedge on one side, gardens on the other,
A no man's land between the town and country.
Teenagers escape here during *Crossroads*
For calf-love, horseplay or a quiet smoke.
They lounge around in boots and faded denim
Like cowhands in a sunset on a Western.
Their bikes lie in the grass, the handlebars
Horns on a herd of new metallic cattle.

## Horse

A horsebox parked by a Land Rover,
A blue saloon car with its hatchback open,
One sunlit afternoon in late October
In a paddock neither rural nor suburban.
A handsome pony with a thick blond mane
Is walked in circles past a group of men
Who might be bidding for the horse at auction.
But why the runny bloodstain on its groin?

Where is the foal if that's obstetric blood?
The small pink tube of a mollified erection
Is dangling like a teat and shakes its head,
Though why no mare if he is out to stud?
The wind strips beech trees for the coming winter.
I watch him led round, raw, domestic, neuter.


## Struggle


A blackbird with a split-nib bill
Open wide at an orange angle,

But the beak deformed and the bird dumb,
Strops the lower half on an earthworm.

The mauled intestine of the lawn
Oils a salad of dandelion.

As if excited by writhing meat
The blackbird works with an appetite.

Oh the suffering of them both!
Protracted hunger and slow death.

The worm that will never feel again
Topsoil juicy after rain,

The bird that will never know at all
Berries spherical in his bill,

The answerable mating-call.

37

# Helen

The rape of Helen and the sack of Troy
Began the odyssey of boarding school
With Latin bullying my mother tongue.
My sister, Helen, took a week to die,
My mother said, but I'd have been too young
To learn that in her backbone was a hole.
The bachelor Latin master who could cane
Taught the new Helen to a homesick boy.

And I imagined on the Trojan mound
A rampart crippled like a malformed spine
Round the cremated body of the town,
And when the Trojans saw the empty plain
Or Menelaus heard that she had gone,
Their legendary sorrows spoke for mine.

# Two Dreams

In the first an adder,
One foot long and brown,
Basked on hillfort pasture
Drought had done to a turn,
As I walked with my daughter
Around the dairy farm.

The other dream was odder:
I knew the woman's son;
I was his English master

And I had met her once.
Now we discussed her future
Over a buffet lunch.

The snake moved like a ripple.
I panicked for an axe
To sink into its middle—
A flash of blade and sparks
And head and tail would dribble
Writhing on dusty grass.

A Riesling stood on the table,
Lettuce and hard-boiled eggs.
The mother was suicidal:
Divorce was on the cards.
But as she peeled an apple
Had she made a pass?

My face in the shaving mirror
Is implicated still:
What Joseph said to Pharaoh
Or Jung and Freud reveal
Can never root out my horror
Of the serpent or the girl.

## Catch

A spider's web has trapped a wasp,
The denier of the net has sheared,
The angry buzz has caught a lisp,
The broderie has grown a beard.

A claw in her mosquito net,
The fierce cocoon is snarling loud.
The killer tangled in a knot
Stabs the gossamer of his shroud.


## Nude

The door is open and yes she is naked,
The blonde at the basin cleaning her teeth.
I and her toothbrush are over-excited;
I could catch her quivering rump and eat it
Now as she steps through the steam to the bath.

Her skin wears a two-piece of next to no suntan.
And striped in brown and orange (just like mine)
A flannel, saving energy for later,
Floats in the warm promiscuous water.
Soap and flannel are lucky men.

Sweat on the mirror. Soap in its slime.
Waters have issued, the plughole has moaned
And the bath is empty except for the scum,
The dead hairs, puddle and dirty rim.
She was on two counts not a real blonde.


## Fatso & Spotty

Do you look like the woman
Loafing on the sand,
With the shot-putter's bosom,
A doughnut in her hand,

40

And a massive bathing costume
Which must have been custom-built
To hide her jumbo bottom
In a pink pelmet of kilt?

Or am I like the weakling
With acne on the brain
Diffidently cycling
Uphill against the rain,
Hair lank with natural greases,
Lips mouthing a teenage grudge,
Grim old-fashioned glasses,
Face a pustular smudge?

If he is not my double
And you are not obese,
Why are we both unable
To let such questions cease?
Would Fatso or Spotty
Like to hear the truth?
You have a perfect body
If I am a spotless youth.

## Politics of Envy

In the Jackdaw folder of 'Historical Genitalia',
The suitors of Elizabeth and reasons for their failure,
The Bonsai quality of Buonaparte's regalia,
What Hitler was missing in the region of Westphalia
Would all be investigated *inter* many *alia*.

Elizabeth I in a miniature by Hilliard
Scanned for masculinity by Hotson, Rowse and
 Tillyard,
The gusset of Napoleon expounded like *The Iliad*,
Hitler in his bunker playing pocket billiard
Would all be reproduced by the chiliad or milliard.

But if the young princess's *pudenda* were like Alice's
And only redetermined by Elizabethan malices,
If Buonaparte's was small because he owned huge
 palaces
And Hitler lost a ball when he gave the globe paralysis,
Do malicious jealousies provide all phallic fallacies?

# MICHAEL HOFMANN

## 1967–1971

for R. H.

I lived in an L-shaped room. my chair was
almost directly behind the door, so that,
when I was sitting in it, I was virtually
the last thing in the whole room to be seen.
visitors would have to describe a small
circle in order to face me, crouching
on my chair with a book. early one evening
I read most of *David Copperfield*, put it
down for supper, and never finished it.
sometimes, out of nostalgia, I would read
the stories in a children's encyclopaedia,
flicking past the hundreds of pages of
science and travel and other matters
that separated these islands of fiction.
it was the time I was interested in art,
even in abstract painting. my red jumper
and my blue trousers were my favourite
clothes; and least my brown trousers and
lemon-yellow pullover. my last beating
took place then as well, just before lunch.
I had thoughts of resistance, but decided
to let it go; it was somehow understood
that this would be the last time.

## Calm and Reasonable Complaint

The fourth day of the year must have
Marked the beginning of our new way of life.
For lunch there was curried dragon.
It will all take some getting used to.


## La Nuit Américaine

Her mother was her father's senior by
something like twenty years; a difference
she was proud of. Most recently she was tall,
shapely, and engaged to her date at home,
though still our age and not yet twenty.
A shimmering girl with polished nails and
a soft creamy face, who washed her white
blonde hair with pink strawberry shampoo.
When she was little, her hair caught fire
and her older sister poured water over her.
After that it was short for a while.
There is a photo of her with my sister,
both in pajamas with powdered faces long
past bedtime, leaning against the radiator
like geisha girls. One afternoon after school
we watched a voodoo movie at her house
and I had bad dreams for months afterwards.

(My teenage father kept opening the door
to a bad-tempered old woman with an axe.)

## Entropy (The Late Show)

A split screen, the dream of the early cineastes,
who rounded on their audiences and assaulted them
with pandemonium in a dip- or triptych, shooting
that all-time favourite, the end of the world.
Screaming crowds ensured a box-office success.
People paid to watch themselves and their own
futuristic hysteria in the huge convex mirrors
held up to them in the cinemas of the avant-garde.
They are the antecedents of today's disaster movie
(especially blooming in Japan), and also of this:

a game of darts. On the right half of the screen,
completely expressionless, the pot-bellied players.
Standing like storks on one leg, they lean forward
behind their heavy throwing-arm. Some of them use
a little finger as a telescopic sight. They practise
six or seven hours a day. . . . On the left, in close-up,
their target, treble twenty. With the best of them,
the margin of error is an eighth of an inch, a letter
in type.
                Hating numbers, they rattle down to zero.


## Alone

Through clouds of sawdust and amid metro-
nomic applause, the single brown spotlight
wilts. I get up from my ringside seat,
somewhere in Central Europe, scurrilous
but comparatively immaculate in my

47

Tails and top-hat, Whip and waxed moustaches,
and invite my lions, all of whom are
permanently defaced by strange blemishes,
to sit up on the tubs of their choice:
(Ladies and gentlemen!)


## Sans-Souci

(L. at 22)

Laforgue in Berlin, the kitten among the pigeons.
Occupying a wing in the Palace of Princesses,
his ground-floor suite has as much furniture
as a showroom, but is still capacious. Uruguayan,
the second of eleven children, he is tickled with
his mute servant, who guesses his every wish.

When the army performs on the boulevard outside,
the whole Court crowds into Laforgue's study:
the officers are mad acrobats with monocles.
Laforgue is *French Reader* to Queen Augusta,
the septuagenarian Empress, francophile almost
to the point of treason, and a real nigger
in the blood-and-iron woodpile of Bismarck's Germany.

Laforgue has a Frenchman's eye for the good points
of the old ladies in waiting; and gets practised
at skipping the dirty bits of epistolary novels.
In his free time, he smokes blond cigarettes,
falls for all the bareback riders at the circus,
and entertains 'ardent fantasies of underclothes'.

*Note.* I would like to acknowledge David Arkell's *Looking for Laforgue: An Informal Biography*.

## Carnal Poem

Birds came and pecked at
a group of yellow bread crusts
scattered on a low roof.

She lay on her belly on the
floor, sneakered feet in the air,
copying reproductive systems.

## Incident from Antiquity

As Venus bends forward, a nipple peers
over the top of her purple dress. This is
the only casualty from grief's long-jump,
that has left her on parted knees in the sand—
for otherwise there is not a hair out of place
in her matronly coiffure, piled high and
fixed with a cool white rose with the dew
still on it. As usual, a cherub is at her side,
rubbing crumbs of gold from his permanently
tired eyes with dimpled baby knuckles.
There is no blood, just a suggestion of it
in the red folds of Adonis' silky tunic.
His beautiful hair (her favourite plaything)
is swept clean off his face in a straightforward
manly way that would have pleased him;
it always used to interfere with his hunting.
He is sprawled across his pikestaff—an
unfortunate anachronism—looking as healthy
as a carbon monoxide corpse. A wild boar goes off
into the shade, in search of peace of mind.

## After the Summer

She spoke Austrian and American
and was on her way to Philadelphia—
home to her father, and back to high-school
where the boys can all drive, and leave campus
during free periods. Leaving her mother
alone outside Salzburg, and her boy-friend,
a passionate admirer of *Kaiser Franz-Josef.*
She showed me his photograph, a simmering
obsessive with archaic whiskers and cropped
fair hair that looked white. . . . A doctor
of philosophy at twenty, she tells me,
and a Jesuit about to take orders.
Two years ago he wanted five children with her.
Now he's throwing it all up for the church;
lecturing in church-law at Vienna,
and keeping only a few hundred *schillings*
pocket-money out of his salary.


## Hausfrauenchor

'She's younger than I am, almost certainly
blonde, and he sleeps with her once a year. . . .
The occasion is the office-party—alcohol,
music, and their formal routine collaboration
suddenly becomes something else.—All over
the country, wives write to the agony columns
for advice. One letter covers thousands
of cases. Of course, you want to allow him

his bit of fun; after working all year for
Germany's *Wirtschaftswunder* and your own.
And it's probably more than you can provide
with your cooking, your meat-and-two-veg sex,
the occasional *Sauerbraten* . . . He deserves it.
The rest of the time, he's faithful to you.
But when he comes home at some godforsaken hour,
lipstuck and dishevelled, drunk as a god, his
dried sperm crackling and flaking in his pants,
then you feel differently about it. You wish
you'd gone to the party and kept an eye on him.
—But then the newspapers don't recommend that:
husbands resent it—what's your business
in an office where you never set foot otherwise?
They tell you the only course is to declare
a general amnesty for this particular offence.
A mass-exemption, like the students of '68,
who no longer have a "past", and instead hold
positions in the civil service: vetting radicals;
checking over photographs of demonstrations,
signatories on petitions; looking for traces
of the ineradicable red paint that is sprayed
over crowds of Communists to identify them . . .
So the best way to kill them is with kindness.
—And it isn't any easier for the secretary:
because she doesn't want to be a cock-teaser,
she gets into trouble with her boy-friend. . . .
A week or two later, she gives my husband a tie
for Christmas. The whole family (himself
included) make fun of it, a silly pattern,
awful colours, what a useless garment anyway . . .
But then he wears it all the following year.'

## Back Numbers

Carelessly we tore our love
Like soft newspapers with feet.
Then stooping down, we read
With interest   some vintage items.

## To a Classics Professor

(1806)

'Years ago you were just a poor student.
Until your professor took you under his wing;
he lodged you, found small jobs for you to do,
helped you in your idealistic clashes with
the authorities, completed your education.
When he died, the ghost of gratitude prompted
you to marry his widow, adopt his children.
—You might as well have married your mother.
Now you've become a professor, a public
servant with two consultation hours per week—
you put away your pipe if a student objects—
spending your Sundays on the dictaphone
to your secretary, organising next week's
correspondence. I don't know what I see in you.
You criticise my passionate letters, then
burn them for safety. In return, you write me
Latin tags, stoical philosophy boiled dry.
I placed a knife under my white left breast

(which you've never seen), broke the skin
and sent you my heart's blood on a handkerchief.
You always feel sorry for your wife. Think
of yourself for a change. . . . When my body
is washed up round the next bend in the river,
will that remind you of Tom Sawyer?'


## Lord B. and Others


Yoghurt and garlic-pills, Balkan products
that feed on the myth of immortality
in South-Eastern Europe; based on
the continuing survival of generations
of gypsy violinists and fortune-tellers
born before the birth-certificate.
A weather-beaten old gent on a poster
in a chemist's shop; glaring; below him,
his ambiguous life-enhancing statement:
'It's not how old you are that matters,
it's how old you feel.' Crossing the Alps,
the spectre of Shelley's sister-in-law
following him, pregnant with his child,
Byron stopped at an inn and surrendered
his passport; then entered name and address
on the printed form, giving his age as
'a hundred'. When he died, eight years later,
still only thirty-six, his heart and brain
were accordingly found to be quite used up—
'those of an old man', a devout particular
in his French romancier's biography.

## Point of No Return

One day, without any warning, he wrote
his first poem as an old man. It was
that apparent. No longer the unsatisfied
curiosity of his senses, but an announcement
of tepid matters that didn't excite him.
If it had urgency, it was that of advice.
The state of things in a provincial capital,
not a breathless despatch from the frontiers.


## Fürth i. Wald

for Jan and Anja T.

There are seagulls inland, extensive flooding
and a grey sky. A tractor stalled in midfield
between two goals. Mammoth sawmills collecting trees
and pulping them for furniture and wallpaper . . .
These strips of towns, with their troubled histories,
they are lost in the woods like Hansel and Gretel.
Counters at peace-conferences, they changed hands
so often, they became indistinguishable, worthless.
Polyglot and juggled like Belgium, each of them keeps
a spare name in the other language to fall back on.
Only their wanton, spawning frontier tells them apart,
an arrogant line of wire in an electric clearing.
(A modern derivative of the civic myth of Thebes:
the oxhide cut into ribbons by cunning estate-agents
and laid end-to-end; so many towns called Cuernavaca . . .)
—At other frontiers, it may be a long tunnel instead,
too long for you to hold your breath. At halfway,

the texture of the concrete changes, and the lights,
but you can't say where it is brighter or safer . . .
Nations are irregular parcels, tight with fear.
But their contents have settled during transport.
*Grenzflucht.* Perimeters that are now deserted and
timid, the dream-wrappings clash with each other.
On one side, the lonely heartless villas of the guards.
Dustbins stored like sandbags outside barrackrooms.
The play of searchlights . . . On the other, *Der Neue
Tag* dawns only twice a week nowadays. With its
Nazi-sounding name and millenarian ideals, still
holding the fort for a dwindling readership . . .

## Gruppenbild ohne Dame

1923, gathering Depression. In this interior
in Cologne, it's Laocoön all over again.
This time, Fate has left him his two boys
and taken his wife.—Though it is difficult
to see how a woman could have fitted in, here:
a road winding in an empty landscape on the wall,
the threadbare carpet, and one hard Sunday chair.
. . . A male Trinity, the Father and his two Sons.
The maculate conceptions of his bald head.
Baby watch-chains like Papa's, and knickerbockers
aspiring to the condition of his three-piece suit.
Their knotty skulls show a family likeness,
heads shaved for lice and summer—skinny boys
with their mother's big eyes and hurt mouth.

## Looking at You

### (Caroline)

Having your photograph on my bedside-table
is like having a propeller there . . . My friend
did his project on the Gallipoli Offensive—
with a proud Appendix of family heirlooms:
irrelevant fragments of German aircraft.
I covered the Russian Revolution (the only
lasting consequence of the Great War, I
argued) but with nothing more tactile than
a picture section—central feeding in
Tsarist times: cabbage soup and black bread,
the Eisenstein-faced peasants with red pupils . . .
I take your unnaturally serious expression
and coax it into a smile or a glum look—
dotted lines pencilled in for velocity—but
you still won't budge. Then I imagine your
stasis as whir, movement in perfect phase,
just before it starts walking backwards . . .
All the walks here lead into the autobahn;
they are dual carriageways for pedestrians,
with wire bridges over traffic unusually
quiet in the snow. A blue signpost marks
the distances: Nürnberg 100; Würzburg
(home of the Volkswagen) 200; Berlin 500 . . .

The pioneers of aviation were never alone—
they named their machines after their loved ones.

# MEDBH McGUCKIAN

## The Truth Room

If I were to plant a tree in my handkerchief
Of a garden, it would be a tree of heaven
Which will grow in ash or gravel—like the jewelweed,
Its roots will travel stone, its seeds
Fall fast in a still room. There would be no danger
In our paths thus crossing, it will never come
To resemble me, my cousin of a touch-me-not,
It does not suppress its buds till such
Untimeliness, it takes the cold to break them.

I would want it to bring its moods with it,
Whether it is given to branching low, its branches
Given to wandering. Without trees
I am a moon-walker, I feel breezes
When the whole world is becalmed, in an
Unbreathable sky. From some secret place
Where colour troubles me, I shake a yellow dust.
And yet the very heart of a tree is dead,
Its life is all on the surface, if air reaches it

It leaves the centre hollow and each stage
Of wrapping gone sleepy, as they say of pears,
With rottenness. Still it bends its dead heart
To the light, it is this death that supports it,
Growing harder, as a frozen cloud, dilute
Or buoyant, wills itself to sleep,
Turning inside out, inventing its own sweetness.
It will be to everyone's relief when it starts
Asserting itself, we can't avoid the feeling

It is only really there if it's covered with flowers,
Though frivolity comes easy only to the almond

In a countryside not prone to femininities:
And their prettiness depends on such deceitful
Summers, they leave their ends ajar like naked
Eggs or fecund eyes, while the tree keeps resting
All its nervy, hapless leaves. Its foliage
Always looks as if it has been slept in;
One couldn't call that brown a festive colour:

But unless the purpose of fruit is just
To distance itself, or be crushed, one must wait
Four seasons to see a place, how leaf-fall sums it up.
Then I would call my house 'Falling Water',
Like a truth room where my symptoms feel at home;
And the city's early spring might make a freedom
I thought I had averted stir within me,
With its streets of seeding cloud, its sky's
Plump countrifiedness, blue as God intended.


## Six Road Ends

As optimistic as a five-year diary
This flowering currant, or flourishing corn,
I've potted in the coal-vase. Since
Our marriages we've all filled out,
Our weight problems ballast on the raft
Of our expectancies, even at the end of the month.

But I only believe the potato's heart
Is white when I cut, and the perfume
Of the woollens programme trembles on the clothes
    horse,
Depending so closely on the flexible scenes
Of Kamikaze birds at Six Road Ends
Out of the Mediterranean snow-blue sky.

## The Sitting

My half-sister comes to me to be painted:
She is posing furtively, like a letter being
Pushed under a door, making a tunnel with her
Hands over her dull-rose dress. Yet her coppery
Head is as bright as a net of lemons, I am
Painting it hair by hair as if she had not
Disowned it, or forsaken those unsparkling
Eyes as blue may be sifted from the surface
Of a cloud; and she questions my brisk
Brushwork, the note of positive red
In the kissed mouth I have given her,
As a woman's touch makes curtains blossom
Permanently in a house: she calls it
Wishfulness, the failure of the tampering rain
To go right into the mountain, she prefers
My sea-studies, and will not sit for me
Again, something half-opened, rarer
Than railroads, a soiled red-letter day.

## Hands

The hands of children are like mirrors:
I have watched you searching for yourself
As though you almost still believed
You might make a career out of living;

When it rains and there's nothing for you
To do, you have opened his palm
Where plenty of light falls, despite
His fretting to be left alone,

As if a 'body bruised' 'could please the soul'
With feelings deeper than fairness—
All his homage is not enough
To put you in a class by yourself,

Or make you mind your business, calling
It love. I know your full-blown
Hand is not that of a businessman—
Its sloping heartline indicates

A gambler, one difficult to live with,
Requiring as many virtues in a wife
As there are stars; while I possess
The most beautiful, most unfortunate

Hands, the sudden breaks, the
Little droopings of a woman
Unsuited for motherhood—
How our love-life curves

Its satisfaction through our strange
Domestic situation, its recurrent fever
Never more than a blemish separating
Our earlier and later heavens.

And the child is my hold on you,
When you complain how women
Get together to complain
How women get together:

Travelling the shape of this organ
We are born with, its chains
And mounts will tell my daylight reader
I am not really a city girl at heart.

## To My Grandmother

I would revive you with a swallow's nest:
For as long a time as I could hold my breath
I would feel your pulse like tangled weeds
Separate into pearls—the heart should rule
The summer, ringing like a sickle over
The need to make life hard. I would
Sedate your eyes with rippleseed, those
Hollow points that close as if
Your eyelids had been severed to
Deny you sleep, imagine you a dawn.
I would push a chrysanthemum stone
Into your sleeve without your noticing
Its reaching far, its going, its returning.
When the end of summer comes, it is
A season by itself: when your tongue
Curls back like a sparrow's buried head,
I would fill your mouth with rice and mussels.

## Housemaid's Knee

My spotless flat supplies no information, a haven
Of dried grasses, sisal carpets, of my able body's
Bondage to the romance of utter homemaking, its
Fear of market-places—how I'm happier when lost
In my busy living-room, than prising crayfish under-
water,
Catching possum, clubbing seals, in such decaying
groves,
At night my child would be her father's bedfellow,
By day ride on his back to the island of canoes.

She's my stuffed toy, I pin and deck her out
In tulip sleeves and sweetheart necklines, the affectionless
Tyranny of dolls who like between their legs
A smooth unbrokenness that lets them be
The stimulus of care, their only errand
The marasmus of their chiselled breasts.


## The Heiress

You say I should stay out of the low
Fields; though my hands love dark,
I should creep till they are heart-shaped,
Like Italian rooms no longer hurt by sun:

When I look at the striped marble of the glen,
I see the husbandry of a good spadesman,
Lifting without injury, or making sure
Where the furrow is this year, the ridge
Will be the next; and my pinched grain,
Hanging like a window on the smooth spot
Of a mountain, or a place for fawns, watches
Your way with horses, your delicate adam work.

But I am lighter of a son, through my slashed
Sleeves the inner sleeves of purple keep remembering
The moment exactly, remembering the birth
Of an heiress means the gobbling of land:

I tell you, dead leaves do not necessarily
Fall, it is not coldness, but the tree itself
That bids them go, preventing their destruction.
So I walk along the beach, unruly, I drop
Among my shrubbery of seaweed my black acorn
   buttons.

# Gladiolus

This border plant whose stately flowers clone
Their saturated reds on a single stem
Will not exhaust the ground like the bushy dahlia:
Its only aim the art
Of making oneself loved,
It grows in transit with the satiny moons
Of honesty, stepping free even of its own
Foliage, evergreen or evergrey, its collared
Leaves overlying, and its grains ripped
Benignly like so many kernels, like a thousand
Cards shuffled in a roguish draught, to catch
The daughter-cells, the reason for these yellow scars.

# The Snow Poem

The moon is past her sleep: like a little
Ambulance or something very pessimistic,
The promise of a wet summer, she inclines
Her leaded porch at a tangent to the sun
So her true door is always at its darkest.

Its exact colour might have been
A slow honey, all that was natural
And impossible, the elegant seduction
Of the sea, that has no real urge
To touch anything, dreaming of being

In the most peaceful place in the world.
Now the sky is the same colour
As it was when I opened the blinds this morning,
Purring like a harp because
It had rained itself out, such

A victory look it gave me, almost
Over-playful, fearless of the rain
At its heaviest, my paying guest
With whom I have the oddest understanding,
The impoverishment, the going-away hat:

And since I was the only character
Who cried, I hoped her shadow
Might find a cave to sleep in, safer
Than lighthouses, pennywise, the just-
Fallen snowrings just becoming hay.


## The Explanation

It was not as the snow said, forever waving
Explanatory arms, explaining nothing: all day
I dreamt about the flutter of your wrists, your
Left-handedness that fled at dawn
Before her silverpoints could clear away
My fantasy of one-day storms.

Perhaps ill-mannered is too strong a word,
And yet it has softly rooted in my head,
Like the weather that builds up at your gate,
The scolding weather of seagulls, what
A slow-moving couple we are, how
I might as well be dead

As try to match such candour—not until
A house is unmistakably relinquished
Will tomorrow's wind recall the glorious
Summer of our installation, rooms
That never liked velvet the suffocating
September of our moving-in.

## The Flower Master

Like foxgloves, in the school of the grass moon,
We come to terms with shade, with the principle
Of enfolding space: our scissors in brocade,
We learn the coolness of straight edges, how
To gently stroke the necks of daffodils
And make them throw their heads back to the sun:

We slip the thready stems of violets, delay
The loveliness of the hibiscus dawn with quiet ovals,
Spirals of feverfew like water splashing,
The papery legacies of bluebells—we do
Sea-fans with sea-lavender, moon-arrangements
Roughly for the festival of moon-viewing.

This black container calls for sloes, sweet
Sultan, dainty nipplewort, in honour
Of a special guest, who summoned to the
Tea ceremony, must stoop to our low doorway,
Our fontanelle, the trout's dimpled feet.

## The Sunbench

Behind my party wall what bolts of silk
Prepare their images, relax from them
Like petals lolling in a knot garden
Voluptuous with rapid growth! These seed leaves
I have summered and these true leaves wintered
Through the spartan frost, supported by sweet chestnut,
Riven oak, till lime unlocks their mongrel
Tenderness, the shattering excretion of the rose . . .

This is not the hardness of a single night,
A rib that I could clearly do without—it is
The room where you have eaten daily
Shaking free like a hosting tree, the garden
Shaking off the night's weak appetite,
The sunbench brown and draining into fallow.


## Cologne

The disdain of green summer cloud
On our glasshouses has bred out
The tomato's coat of hair; and a man
Without lice is less virile, seeing
The invisibility of women:

And flowers yield themselves less foolishly
Than deer that fan their perfume
With the affluence of flattened tears:
They must be harvested at dawn, before
Their permafrost has sunk beyond

A skater's melted world,
Rude as hyacinths encircling
A private room at night,
To this tall icicle, my geranium oil,
The spills of my patchoulied cashmere shawl.


## The Theatre


This is our second friendship, recent
And jealous, a treaty cold
As your distrust of music.
Though you understand
Poetry better than men, I trust your tongue
As I would a stone that thirsts after the weather,
Little stay-at-home, living without
Perfecting itself.

You are always hungry, not made
For prison; you have no handwriting
Because you never write—yours is the readership
Of the rough places where I make
My sweet refusals of you, your
Natural violence.

So with the best sort of thankfulness,
I throw the window romantically open
To let sleep out of the room, or the possibility
My poems might have perished. Would
They last even as long
As the sun's burn on your arm?

I do not reproach the sky
For its answer—if you had a boat,
You would name it Socrates, perhaps,
After yourself, and tell me
How I live in poems, or how
Far away I was
In the bad light, on the stage of the summer theatre.


## Waters


In quiet streams, the buoyancy of water-lily leaves
Will take the even weight of a child on their celled floors;
The bamboo dies as soon as it has flowered, however
    scantily,
The sacred lotus opens wide on four successive nights.

A search round fern patches in the autumn will discern
A ribbon or a heart of simple moss that hugs the ground
Where spores have fallen—some have changed their leaves
To roots, and left the shore for the eternal spray of water-
    falls.

Straw-coloured rhododendron trusses seem insensible
To snow, with their felted backs, of tan or silver brown;
The barrel-palm appreciates above its swollen trunk
The neat habits of camellias, the water-loss of dates.

BLAKE MORRISON

## Flood

We live in the promise of miraculous lakes:
Dagenham, Greenwich, Wapping, the Isle of Dogs.

'When the siren sounds, those in the blue environs
Should proceed immediately to non-risk zones.'

Spring tides, high winds: for days we can hear
Of nothing else, our eyes bright with disaster,

Our minds a chronicle of *mountaing anarchie,*
*The river-folke frantick, shippës trappt in trees.*

*And the dove we sent out, when it came back,*
*Had the brown glaze of estuaries on its beak.*

In our dream no sandbags hold back the flood:
We would bring the whole world down if we could.

## The Renunciation

Our lives were wasted but we never knew.
There was such work to be done: the watch-chains
And factories, the papers to sign
In the study. Surrounded by brass
How could we see what we amounted to—
A glint of eyes as headlights swept away?

In a cot on the lawn lies my nephew,
Whose name I can't remember—the strands
Of family thinner each year, though we
Are here again, politely. The sun comes through
Like a faint reminder of things not done:
Forgotten dates, brothers not loved enough.

*Peter, Jenny's husband, never forgave her.*
*When he caught them, out by the links, it was*
*All quite tame—some shouts and blows, Jenny*
*In tears, and the lover not showing again.*
*But later—well Pete really cracked. Jen said he used*
*The affair as a way of opting out of things for good.*

Here, on this stone, a relief map of lichen,
Each mossy headland like a lush green future.
Swallows gather on the wire, darkening
The air with their forked legends—journeys
We planned to take too, had the time been right
And the distance to the airport less far.

Every verse is a last verse, concluding
Sadness. You hear its tone in the chestnuts
And rookery—how much has been taken.
The garden with its nightshade nags like some
Vague guilt and the rooms look so untidy—
But there is nothing we know of to be done.

*Simon has a sperm count of ten million—*
*Almost no chance at all, the clinic said.*
*'Funny those years of worrying if the girl . . .*
*When all the time . . . and now Louise, who'd set*
*Her heart on three . . . there's fostering, true but when . . .*
*I've lost the urge as well—know what I mean.'*

I have learnt lately to admire the traits
Of those who dispossess me: their scars,
Their way of getting straight to the point,
Things mattering. Their families roam the orchards,
At home among the tennis courts and lupins.
I watch—I have resigned myself to light.

Our lives run down like lawns to a sundial,
And unborn children play in a world I imagine
As good: the sash cords run free again
And I am leaning out and calling them
To hurry now and join us quickly, will they,
Quickly—we are all ready to begin.

## Phone

Somewhere a phone was ringing—perhaps for you.
It crooned like a chance that would change the world,
Though the room, when you got there, seemed
    undisturbed,
Dust and sunlight for a hundred years
No noise had ever got under.
It bothered you for a while, but friends came round,
And the summer was a deep, deep blue
That stretched over mountains and marram-grass
And paved terraces with drinks at sunset.
They were beautiful hours, weren't they,
High and open as Alpine fields, where even the cows,
Belled and indolent, sound musical.
You should have forgotten but it came back—
What the voice would say if you got there in time,
Something on a line you did not recognise,
Though the tone seemed familiar and the background
Rushed forward like a shower of bright coins.

Well, you went on: there was no one to say
It would not ring again or in time maybe
That you couldn't dial yourself. These nights draw in,
Misty light fading by four, but the words
At least will be clear and golden when they come,
Like 'Why not meet me?' or 'I forgive you'.


## A Concise Definition of Answers


The city calls with its arches and spires
While the flatlands flourish with incest.
There are more curious things I wanted,
If possible, to touch on today—
How the sky, for instance, on these sultry afternoons,
Seems to settle round your forehead,
Or the link between nostalgia and smell.

At this point science comes in,
As you might expect, or as you might yourself
Come in with that colander of raspberries and rain.
It seems like all we ever hoped for—
As if the mayor had cut the tape
And events might finally begin.

But look, there's a storm blowing up,
The sky flickering like an old TV
And the volume almost deafening. Answers:
I was holding them here just now
But they are gone again into these cloud-lit days
Where martins and swifts sweep low
Over the ground but can turn up nothing.

## Couples

Having no idea how to pass their time together
they invite other couples to dinner,

and take their coats and serve martinis or gin:
yellow clocks an hour short float in them.

What strange communions—wine, candles, bread,
and a host with parables prepared.

What strange food, too—melon smiles, mince rare
in marrows that have lost their hearts, potholed gruyère.

Bored, one diner turns himself over in a spoon.
For his next trick he will disappear in

his hostess's napkin where, if it works as planned,
he'll hold in secret her immaculate hand.


## Stepping in and out of Manet

An untroubled nakedness:
the lady picnics
with these men from the city.

You were gathering violets
then took the rowboat
to the clearing where I waited.

There was a tree with fungi
like a frilly dress
and our lips' first meeting—

that wet little bridge of sighs.
Inhibition fell away
like fruit across the grass.

Older now, you frown as if
it made you sad
to think how dangerous we were

among the woods and cow-parsley,
where the light fell in
and our love was undisturbed.


## Barley


Barley, with that sheen none of the others has
and the slinky little snake-dance.

The centipede with outrageous antennae,
the shaving-brush, the flimsy, upended broom.

From this pathway biblically parting your sea
we observe a sad maturing:

the promise of June, your alert and curious
peering over each other's shoulder, your daft aerials

waiting for some message that will never come.
And then July, your heads sinking lower and lower,

a hum over the fields as tall machines
make their way through a cyclone of chaff.

Only this can flatten you, though love tries too—
its impress where the young lie down together.


## Fuel Debts Enquiry


When I surveyed the wondrous New Cross blocks,
layers of eyes froze behind spyholes.

*I can/cannot afford to heat my living room*:
interviewers circle as appropriate.

The flats massed like an iceberg, nine-tenths in the blue,
strung together by a lift I did not dare to take.

Rung after rung I mounted, trekked down corridors,
hung about for answers twenty floors up.

Inscrutable, screwed to the doors, threshold lenses
telescoped my well-meant profile.

Dogs barked, carpeted steps secretly came and went,
the Cyclops stare guarded all who dwelt in there.

I did/did not establish who was in arrears.
I could get some/no statistics on the coldness inside.

# From *Looking at Tower Blocks*

## I

Ghost-towers, upended coffins
where we bury our living
(the poor, the old, those that don't matter)

what names they have given you
here in the Lewisham wastes:
Hercules and Pegasus and Orpheus,

the mythology of Milton Court Estate.
That you might come alive at night,
as Schopenhauer said all statues do,

and perform brave feats—
was that what they were thinking?
You were carrying their little hopes for them

like giants sent to combat,
or like Lot's family
escaping the darkness of the past.

Pillars of salt, faithless ones,
the fires of atonement
blaze in your windows each dusk.


## II

Huge, never-to-land *Narrenschiff*
becalmed in the estates,
what sad faces stare from your rigging.

There was fever, I'd heard,
in the worst of your cabins,
and occasional mad folk lost overboard.

But now I've seen for myself
these twenty-eight gangways
—and frankly nothing seems right.

How far you've drifted
from Saint-Elia's yard,
his blueprints for a future powered

by vast 'dynamic' fleets.
Grey and unwanted, you float here
in the wake of that dream—

doomed to these wastes forever,
though each morning women come
to hang distress flags from your side.

### III

God's stereo, the tall cabinets
ranged about these towns and estates.

Day after day we wait here like terriers
for our master's voice—

but the speakers stay dumb.
It is the perfect system:

cranes lift and descend
like turntable arms, children

go round in the school-yard.
But where is the word

we were told was arriving,
the great rushing of tongues?

He has bequeathed us silence,
the track of His absence

unwinding its love.


IV

It is your light I love most,
its heaping up at evening
like the candles in Sacre Coeur.

But more rigorous, I suppose,
the way that Mondrian might handle
a stained glass window.

'A machine for living in'
le Corbusier said,
but some of those who followed

wanted soul to be there too.
They were thinking of altars,
tablets raised against the dark,

in whose brilliant oblongs
we could congregate and love.
And though it didn't come to pass

you have that look about you still,
a frail community of light
it hurts to disbelieve in.

## Glass: A Short Biography

Daughter of light, Aunt Cindy's favourite,
with your unblemished skin that children
press their noses up against, and your
sharp little jokes they run from, bleeding.

Brittle virgin, wooed as in old-style plays
by whistling gallants on high ladders:
immodest, you let them see everything,
but survive their attentions intact.

Mother and worker, the seed's catalyst
and the clear-eyed protector of home;
yet unfaithful by night, when drinkers hold you
and perverts meet that self-effacing stare.

Martyress, stoned for unspecified crimes,
your wounds like the star of David;
but radiant in churches as the sun goes down,
or with dust laid over in delicate fronds.


## Theory of Heredity

The generations come down on you—
like football crowds when a goal is scored.

It began when a sperm, waving its scarf excitedly,
tick-ticked its way in through the turnstile.

Now it's reached hundreds—parents, and their parents,
and the ones before that, stacked on the terraces

as high as sight, and you're at the bottom.
And when they heave like corn through the afternoon

you will heave along with them, though you thought
by now you could go which way you pleased.


## Our Domestic Graces

The Chancellor of Gifts is an élitist.
You can't pretend he'll step out of the night
with a gilt invitation-card or flowers.
The brilliant words we wrote down in a dream
aren't there beside our bedside after all.

Yet something calls from the great expanse
of air we have made our latest home in.
Studio voices wake us near eight
with stories of God and how 'He moves
among us like light'. What are his tracks like?

Mystery starts no further away
than these mossy footprints crossing the lawn
to where the raspberries are ripe again
and the panes of the greenhouse brim with tears.
Today even our lost city appears

from its shroud: a white dust-sheet slowly lifts
and here are all our glinting heirlooms—
the gasworks, like a coronet, queens it
over the houses, and bridges grace
the river with their lacy hems and Vs.

To have it all so clear—the congregating
chimney-pots, the lines of traffic passing
over the heath like words being typed on a page.
Christ's fishermen must have felt like this,
crying out, amazed, at their spangled catch.

Light falls about these rooms, silvering the face
of what we are most used to, and ourselves,
who on such days might think we had been
elected at last—guest musicians
at the garden party of the gods.

SIMON RAE

## The Tools

### To John Caperon


But there were also those who merely hauled
The huge blocks up into the creaking rafters;
Who used the scaffold's eminence to startle
The respectable below, shame passing girls;
Saw toil in terms of bread and ale, the chance
To take a woman to the fair and bed
Her afterwards; whose blasphemies and snatches
Of whatever songs were tavern-current brought
Unbruised fingers up to pious lips, and set
Hastily averted eyes to scan
Height's sublimity; whose fractured limbs
Were set as often skew as straight; whose hovels,
Humbled by the labour of their days,
Were never visited when they fell sick;
Who never understood the plan or saw
In their mind's eye the final structure raised,
Nor the relation of the parts to what,
When finally completed, made up more
Than stone on stone piled up to point a spire,
Great walls of storied glass and furnishings
So rich few nobles' halls could bear
Comparison.
                But it was theirs as much
As any bishop's. He worked in them as
He had in those who hammered heavy nails
Through splitting palms and hoisted three small deaths
Against the sky, not thinking what they did,
Nor breaking off to ask each other why.

# Natural Theology

To them, of course, our succulent,
sweat-smeared torsos denote
a Benign Horsefly in the sky,
though our flailings with hands,
the daily news or books
confuse their theologians
with the problem of pain and evil.
The atheistical mock, hovering
at a safe distance—'How
can all be for the best with these
unexplained convulsions of our
given manna? Can we not,
rather, deduce a Wicked Fly
who built that blurred source
of pleasurable smells and promises
simply to destroy the race for his
amusement? And who, anyway, tastes?'
And they weave erratic patterns
on their three-dimensional looms
in their delight at confounding
the optimistic priests of the flesh.
But the believers laugh in reply:
'Few die,' they say, 'and the law
is anyway strict upon
the unnecessarily greedy.'
Then they gather in loose formation
and swing, each a sunbeam,
down to my neck at six o'clock.

## Aubade

Some mornings it's the Court Farm dog,
sawing into the silence rhythmically
like a carpenter aiming into a fresh plank;
on some, it's the cocks they keep
on the allotments up the road from us,
swinging the rusty hinges of their throats,
or another border incident
among the feuding geese. And then
the doves' five-finger exercise begins,
tuneless as a first recorder lesson,
half-echoed by the inane cuckoo's
eponymous call. The woodpecker twangs
its ruler in a desk-lid. When there's
a breath of wind I hear the limes
outside my window shuffling their leaves
in susurrous applause. Sometimes
I'm woken by the bullocks booing,
or by the sheep cursing listlessly—
*merde, merde*—their original grievance
long since forgotten. Occasionally
a tractor tows a clanking skeleton
with rows of cast-iron wheels
like vertebrae up through the village
to rust in the corner of another field
till it's needed to comb a scurf
of stones out of the soil or carve
the stubble over on itself.
But on this morning I come to
to nothing more than sunlight
on half-filled packing cases
and an empty wall, blocked
like a precinct where my pictures hung.

## Frost at Midnight

Leaving the darts grouped
like stiff hairs in a nostril,
he salutes the unhammocked tits
of the brewery's pin-up

and shoulders into the night.
Bladder pulsing like a bag-pipe,
he plays the warm notes
over the hedge's crisp pallor;

they issue in a dark stain
at his splayed, unsteady feet,
which quarrel all the way home.
On the porch he fights the latch

with his boots. Upstairs
he follows the erratic cabaret
the dying fire projects
around his room, his ear pressed

to the radio's lamé crotch,
taut with the city's promises.
The long hunger stirs; he dreams
of summer and distances, speed,

above all, speed, the verge-grass
shimmying like a feather-boa
in the wake of radiant limousines,
unflinching motorbikes. Outside

frost knots in the veins of pipes,
sews its lichen constellations

in the road's black pores, confirms
puddles in a hard virginity.


## *Thaw*

Trees where the cattle shelter
in summer drip like urinals;
later they will unload wholesale,
each dumping a sibilant rush
and its own brittle cushioning.
The pond's cataract is breaking up
and the skates' sky-writing's lapped
by leaking water at the toe's touch.
The stream gargles its sore throat,
dislodging ice-floes of phlegm. Soon
darkness will be returned to dusk,
the shorn trees powerless to prevent
the light ebbing. The lane's
corrugated back will yield to the tyres'
awkward massage, and any last flakes
shaken out of the sky will perish
like the Poles at Arnhem.


## *First Snow*

Birds print their forlorn tunes
on the yard's blank score. I throw
stale from the breadbin. Bobbing
in their quilted straitjackets
they fidget with the crusts.

The bitter beauty glitters—
every branch, stem and stalk
coralled, each a precise statement
of fragility delighting
after December's muddy blur.
But it abrupts all process, itself
the frustration of streams, and there are bales
to be got out into the fields where sheep
send up their baas like flares
above a landscape they are cruelly
camouflaged in. Mid-morning a fox
risks the hot fan of shot, dragged
by wires in his belly to the chickens' compound
and the unyielding zinc of the bins.
Later, a tractor is needed at the end of the lane
where a bend's suddenness is marked
by tyres' wild graffiti, punctuated
by the stop of an up-turned chassis.
At dusk it is the failure of darkness
one notices, the hedges dully luminous,
the earth for once instinct
with a glimmering light. At night,
passing the men's dank holes
on the way to the unwelcoming pail,
I stop to look down on the village,
its one street moon-paved under the stars.


## Countryman

He liked the smell of his new wife
on his fingers all day, or
till it wore off, usurped
by diesel, lost shovelling feed,

or slobbered away by the dogs.
He liked to pretend
when he sat on his tractor
surveying the next field of stubble
to be ploughed under again
he was smoothing his moustache.
It was as insistent as snuff,
better even than the tang
of his gun when he sent the hares
skittering like skimmed pebbles,
or collapsed the labouring flight of a crow
with his coaxing trigger-finger.

## Spring Manoeuvres

Birds wound up like clockwork toys
jerk crazily across the lawn;
one strains at an elastic worm,
anchor-man steady till it frays.

Another alights where a snail
draws its innocent bright smear
along a sleeve of wall, carefully smacks its shell to shrapnel.

A kestrel's sudden lapse from flight,
its precise fall, is terminal.
Through the reverberating dark trawl
the blind expectant acrobat

and the wide-winged stooping cowl,
blotting out the sprinkled stars

of a mouse nailed in the grass,
then climbing back to its patrol.

Underneath night's fluent calls,
stammering gears; what's caught
in the clear cold holocaust of light
by natural reversion falls

in the morning to the crows.
From carious bones of elm
they sail lazily above their realm—
the seedlings' cemetery rows,

the unofficial tip, the road
asterisked with broken fur—
settle, suspecting no danger.
But even the inviolate proud

are subject to the only law
which recognises no defence,
imposing the pellets' sentence
on ingenuous pelt and claw

alike. Stretched between brush and pad
cold carrion views with surprise
a world gone dead, indistinct skies
strangely untenanted.

### Elms

form a gerontocracy superseded
by spring's cadres and outlawed
under the new constitution. One

strikes an oratorical pose, arms
flung aerials of exhortation,
but his rhetoric rots to silence
in his hollow throat. Others
conspire in creaking whispers,
while the completely crazed lie
across the wire, limbs broadcast
in a shatter of rigor mortis.
All are doomed, as their jailor,
the wind, well knows. He likes
to bully them, knocking out
bails of teeth, bending back
brittle fingers just for the fun
of it. And beneath his bluster
the mob's maniac soughing
rises to a snarling crescendo
at each crashing vindication
of a root-and-branch reform.

## Jets

On the other side of the hill
the base is laid out

under its acupuncture course
of early-warning aerials.

Two jets circle the estate
like a couple of athletes

warming up round a perimeter track.
At the opening of a neural hinge

inside a computer they vanish,
towing their surf trails

through the skies of three counties,
to return in ten minutes

as rumours of a torrent
approaching down a conduit,

as a giant's thumb–nail drawn
across the sky's vibrating blackboard

at an impossible velocity.
The elms throw up their hands

in histrionic surrender;
the cattle stolidly continue

drowsing at their moorings
in gently tidal grass.

Stick tucked under his arm
and bending like a skier,

a solitary spy
rests a note-pad on his knee

and scribbles furiously,
one eye cocked to the sky.

# *January: The Drive In*

## for Kate

Starting is a Caesarian operation
involving an umbilical tangle
of jump-leads. We peer anxiously

into the propped wound, faces
masked with the gauze of breath,
hands hugely inhuman in gloves,

persuading with the severally
passed clinking instruments
among the tubes and valves.

We apply healing aerosols
and check the cardiograph again.
The engine shuffles its catarrh

then clears its throat and roars . . .
At the first incline it whinnies,
the whole car threatening to rear,

resisting the foot's firm pressure.
Once clear, we follow the tyres'
rigid consensus till the frozen ruts

give on to the main route's black rink.
An iodine wind sweeps the fine grains
in running drifts like sand

and through this bitter Sahara
an interminable caravan winds.
Some sicken, drop out to form

by nightfall anonymous dunes;
the rest queue nose to haunch
behind lurching tankers easing

their cumbrous bulk down hills
like camels faltering to kneel.
In the suburbs we file past those

left tethered to pavements,
veiled with papers, mouths stopped
with cardboard or foil, bald

craniums skull-capped with snow.
A backed-into radiator grins
through its hare-lip. Ingots

of brown sugar tumble from each
shuddering chassis, roll and spill
into the curranty filling of grit

our wheels strive to kenwood.
Tonight we will drive home through
a landscape of mad confectionery:

plateaus of sandy marzipan,
shifted fortresses of icing
stuck with sodium candles.

# Home Counties May

The gardens open like floral encyclopaedias;
the blossom brims then tumbles on the breeze,
miring the concrete path to the tradesmen's entrance,
littering the lawn with a loveliness everyone takes
for a portent of perfect summer. The chestnuts strain
at their guyropes like enormous marquees. Winter's
    doubts
and shamefaced consultations are forgotten, the medicines
left to harden and crack in the bathroom cupboard.
She looks his short-sleeved shirts out,
watching the gardener's disembodied head
bobbing above a wall, enjoying the comforting chatter
of the lawnmower, the aroma of freshly cut grass.
Later, he hears through the open study window
her secateurs tut-tutting among the rose-bushes.
The wasps have not yet arrived, and the long vista
opens before them—a sort of painless convalescence
in deckchairs, a hand hanging down to mute
crackling applause from Lord's or Wimbledon,
a library romance neglected on the lap
as the eyes follow the intricacies of the sprinkler
executing a lazy *pas de seul*, while the ears
are tickled by the plucking of tennis and the bathers'
distant cries. Neither foresees the days when the clouds
will haemorrhage, and the rain pull the peonies
to pieces, leaving their petals like the remains
of a pigeon picked over by the cat on the lawn,
nor dreams of the drifting corpse's slack embrace
or the punt's elusive painter trailing in the shallows
below the derelict boathouse; nor spares a thought
for summer's close and the importunate squat figure
sculling across the darkening waters of the reservoir.

## Wet March

Streams have a new-found importance,
bustling through culverts with telegrams
of dead leaves, disintegrating parcels
of sticks and sacking. In the woods
where elms lean like wrecked wickets
amidst discarded pads of bark,
you can hear the echo of yesterday's rain
dripping on to autumn's ruined carpet.
It lies exhausted in the fields, or here,
in the lane's parallel ruts, the colour
of forgotten tea. Sounds come differently
through this laden atmosphere: shots
in the spinney reverberate like a door
with a glass pane repeatedly slammed.
They are thinning the rookery.
A terrified jeering flares up, then
dies away. I picture a broken Icarus
running the gauntlet of whipping spray
to rest among wishbones of twig, claws
crooked in a final, fierce petition.
A chain-saw moans like distant motor-cross,
gears gagging at the impossible gradients
the years have packed into the condemned
timber's grain. It starts to rain again,
pocking the stale pats the cattle dropped,
infiltrating the hoof-holed turf
where the hunt drummed through a gateway.
I notice a single print from the spoor
ringed like a fairground prize by a quoit
of horseshoe, and turn up an inadequate collar
as the landscape blinks into tears
on the other side of my glasses.

# JOE SHEERIN

## Rescuing a Princess

After the thunder of falling giant,
After the rutted ground, the scaled wall
And the forced door, she having measured
The to and fro of clashing shield, trembled
At the fall and read the silence, knew
Before lock was broken what to expect.
So long out of sunlight she cowered
At the bright day, the glare of turned ground,
The flame of new wounds demanding as lips.

He examined his prize in full light. Her
Hair after a good wash would fall flaxen
To her hips; her face perfect, almost, and enough
Of her breast visible to attract a man
With an exploring mind. He licked his wounds

And seeing in her face of horror a small
Tongue of pity was man enough to realise
That in the solitude of the long nights in the interval
Between battles something must have happened.
Brute or lover in bed, one must survive.

And helping her on to his horse whispered. I know
What went on and ask only that you look back
Once innocent-faced. Beyond the page the children
Are already besieging you with their pure passion.

# Dwarfs

When the dwarfs came home,
Their mannikin hands calloused
And their pockets full of ripe diamonds,
Singing like streams and marching
On short legs quick as love,

They fell upon the neat house
Entering the yellow shaft of door
The brightness of window; children
Around a mother-lover, their
Ears like cattle and faces
Common as warts.

She, dressed simple as a
Tree, having sent the cuddly
Things of daylight to their beds,
Spread her dainty love like
Butter on their flat skulls.

They sat, small male chauvinists
Around the plank table and smelled
Her kitchen smells. She tripped
With dishes, some hot as soup and
Some, galling as aphrodisiacs
On their nobodies.

Afterwards, their bellies clogged
And their heads swimming in
Admiration, she danced tactful
As an ankle and sang, words of syrup
In the gathering air. They longed.

The fire ebbed. The bats of
Night came out. Their elf
Eyes read the future in the falling
Ash. First a witch and then a prince.

The apple of hate they forgave. But
The kiss, the kiss sucked the breath
From their small lungs.

## Persephone

Expectant after the long winter the fallow
Garden lay swollen with rain. The gardener,
Careful as a midwife, shaved the weeds clean;
Lit a fire and hunkered beside it to wait.
A few days later, in response perhaps to a
Passable sun, some movement was discernible
Underground. The butting of a head. He drew

The screens, keeping curious girls and sniggering
Youths away, obscured the view. The first
Crack appeared over near the bushes. He lalaed
Encouragement, sunk a graip in the ground and eased
The earth apart. It was early days yet and the task
Of birth takes patience. The tear widened. Deep
Earth, smelling of core metal, dribbled out. Then

A head; the hair muddied but undeniably female.
'We have a crown. Careful now with the graip.'
Her head came in a rush, eyes blackened with soil,
Nostrils and ears plugged with roots, mouth streaked
With slime. This was the crucial moment. He
Lunged forward, forced her lips apart and sucked.

He spat out mouthfuls of mucus and mud. She
Grasped for air as he eased back lips of earth.
Her shoulders broke ground, breasts stained dark,
But firm as apples. Her waist was slender as a fish.
He pulled, hooking her under the armpits, panting.
Her hips held an instant, until she slithered free
And lay on the grass heaving lungfuls of air.

He had the hose ready and watched the water whiten
Her body in circles. He lathered and rinsed her hair.
She stood classically upright for the final dousing
Down. Too exhausted he dried her carefully without
    passion.

It was time to show her off now. He opened the screens
And stood in the warmth of the admiration. There was
An intaking of breath, a yearly remembering of what
It is like. All this time she stood strange and apart,
Head sideways, and ears pricked for the first sound
Of music, carried invisibly as scent, on the wind.


## A Study in Charcoal

When the quick fire ransacked the school I
Hurried there, my hair raging in the rancid
Wind; not caring that my breasts bellied out
From under my blouse or that my fierce panting
Drew uncouth stares from the passers by.

All dead said the white-haired master as gentle
As a priest. But I searched unbelieving,
Turning charred desks with my blistered hands,
Stepping over ragged bodies or kneeling
Mothers pressing their dead in desperation.

Among the sobs my sharp ears pricked one I knew,
Coming from an outside closet behind a locked
Door. I forced it open and he stood there
Roundly alive. Asked me to do up his flies.

I seized him and carried him like a monstrance
Through the blackened rubble. On each side they
Parted holding their charred bundles like fiends.
I'm damned if I could share their sorrow, my
Whole body singing, this is a happy day.


## A Cup of Tea

After months of silence my neighbour knocked.
I presented my eye interrogatively at the peep
Hole and waited. My child, she said, is dead.
I was cagey, aware it might only be a ruse
To open a conversation. Which one? My eyebrow
A horizontal question mark. The one with golden
Hair, blue enamel eyes and porcelain cheeks.
Prove it, I demanded. My kettle was boiling over.

She demagnified and I measured some tea into a pot.
Again she knocked and I offered my eye. True
She held an infant but hard to ascertain whether
Sleeping or dead. I am a cautious person. I
Ordered a mirror and a feather to be brought.

She offered feather and mirror to his lips.
It was a blustery day and I couldn't be sure.
Tickle him, remembering how a tickled child
Twitches in sleep. He made no movement. I
Wasn't convinced. More, more. Under the armpit.

She played walkie-round-the-garden and this-
Little-piggy with his rigid limbs. No smile
Broke the piety of his face. He's dead I conceded.
What am I to do she asked? a sculptured tear
On her face. Call a doctor and get a death
Certificate. You will need this for the Registrar
Of Deaths. Inform an undertaker stipulating a small
Coffin. You have a choice of consecrated ground or
A crematorium. Contact tax or social security or both.

My tea was drawn and she, I suppose, went home. I
Could have set a precedent and asked her in but she
Has seven more children and my own flesh was dying
Even as she spoke.


## The Leman

The letter I wrote you in invisible ink
Clarifies my love. It will betray its message
Having first been soaked in lemon—one
Stolen from a market stall should suffice—
And gently heated by your breath. Do not kiss
Or place it under your armpit. Keep some distance.
And remember it will not yield to milk or whey.

Fallen into the wrong hands an unmarked sheet
Means no love lost. Let them disbelieve.
Having read the message and understood, destroy
Like a good agent, the evidence. Ball tightly
In your fist and eat tearing word from word.
Swallow completely before continuing your walk.

Try not to wince remembering it's the bitterness
Of the lemon's nature that's at fault not my words.


## The Confession


She took me to the wood at night.
It was damn cold and a drizzle crossed
The moon's face and daubed our coats.

Under blackthorn, low enough to make
Us sink our heads, and where tins rusted
Delicate as scabs, she motioned me to wait

Like a priest and whispered in my
Face what had pushed sleep from her
Head those last days and nights and

Made her bite her guilty lips and wash
Her body until it ached. She said
She had, being lonely and unloved, broken

Seals. That was too dramatic I said
Call a spade a spade. She let fall
Some tears to join the rain and said she made

Love to a man who sold used cars, not
Love but lust and felt ashamed. She waited
Open-lipped for penance or absolution but I

Only cursed the rain that damped the moon
And made the journey home all wet and gloom.

## Playing Soldiers

The plants are on the move. Their scouts
Have already pierced our defences and
Settled themselves solidly in pots on vantage
Points around the room, on window sills,
Sideboards and table tops. They command each landing.

At first one or two only sat obediently,
Dull of leaf and sipped water once a week.
They showed no ambition and knew their place.
This ploy won our confidence over.

Others sneaked in after dark, settled behind
Us, while we played toy soldiers on the carpet.
They grew stealthily and were docile to touch,
Licking our hands and stroking our necks eagerly.

That was the signal for an all-out assault.
Spores and parachuting seeds tapped at the window
Panes. The lawn flexed its battalions and the
Back garden nuzzled at the door.

Inside the chairs and tables are restless,
The crucified doors groan and upstairs the
Floors heave in their winter of discontent.
We play silently now in the narrowing circle of floor.

People who call remark on our green fingers, our
Apple cheeks, while the plants nod waiting until
Defenceless our roots penetrate the carpet and concrete
    under.

# A Ghost's Life

The maximum age of a house ghost is
Five hundred years. After that they
Pack their shroud and fuck off
To other places without walls or

Stairways or hedges or sunken lawns.
They've done their porridge, floating
Across old ground, bending over cots,
Fading through walls and making hackles
Rise with their behind presence.

Perhaps then they go to factories, sit
Under groaning pipes, pass through lathes,
And sulk in cold canteens until sun-up.
Or hang over railway bridges like tramps,
Or spit into rivers, or loiter outside
Closed shops, until the first bus pierces
The dawn; then fade silent as darkness.

What happens then is pure speculation. Some
Say they return, hitch a likely spermatoza,
Steer it to an egg, sit at anchor, make eyes,
Sprout limbs of blood, kick the hostess
Mischievously from the inside, butt
Downwards with the head, break out, scream.

# Loki

The god of mischief rules. He sends some,
Without minds, roaring through corridors,
Careering against chairs, crashing foreheads
Against brick. They laugh like thunder and only
Ever threaten to use their cocks in anger.

Young women, equipped like Venus, are
As open as petticoats. They dribble smiles
And stroke their thighs; or expose tits
They can never hang an infant on.

Others with minds as nimble as music, he
Imprisons in diseased bodies that wither
From the toes to the neck. The heads
Are the last to die, helpless as rabbits.
They know the gentleness of hand on
Breast and the love that passes understanding.

He removes the spines of some children
In the womb and mocks others in play
Grounds, legs laden like scrapyards.
He pokes out eyes and bites off tongues
And twists heads round to face the shoulder.

Of course we fight him with drugs and
Calipers and prayer and talking dogs and Health
Acts and small pensions and public sympathy
And toilets chromed like thrones. But he
Always wins again with some new trickery.

# The Lover

Early in spring my father went courting
Death's daughter. He shaved a blush
Into his thin jaw, slyly went for walks
Alone at dusk. We observed them dimly
Behind hedges, heard them whisper in the barn.
His face was damp and his meat often lay
Untouched on his plate. We sensed romance.

Hurtful after his solid faithfulness; his stubbled
Kisses and his quiet words were sacraments
(love had his small-meshed net about our house then),
Not easily spat out or renegued on in the night.

Exhausted from watching we dozed inevitably
And he eloped into the blustery night with
No moon and the scutching wind on his thin
Nightdress. He woke up deceived. In a single

Bed in a dark church I saw him last lying. A candle
Winked and I recognised her passionless eye
And her hair wisping like roots around the pillows.

That night I kissed my children greedily, held
My wife close, promised love for ever. An old
Vow, Somehow, by God, I meant to keep it.

# Digging

Late in September Agnes came into heat.
We noticed it first over a strained breakfast
Noted how she aimed her words at distance and
Her eyes bright beyond morning burned.

Fearing death in every corner and cupboard
We suspected fever, smoothed her damp hair
Back and wound her carefully in a blanket.

The petty morning took its toll of our attention
And she unwrapped herself from silence.
Our eyes next found her on the green at
The street's end. Unmistakable her flat bent

Chest and convict's leg among the pressing
Herd of children. Her uncouth bray rasped
Through our dusted house. We winced each time.

A follower always, she was left behind the
Angled bicycles or watched wild boys scale
The high red wall into the tangled field.

Alone she didn't return to us restlessly pacing
A slow uneven circle on the green, her toecap
Pulling at wet leaves and grass like a small blunt plough.

Frightened as children we watched her through
The leaded panes as she rubbed and rubbed and
Rubbed, a furrow wider than we could jump.

## Backcloth

The day I left home it showered. Some from
Clouds and some from under brows heavy as
Thunder. An oblique sun lit my departure
And picked out autumn on the declining trees.

A bit-part actor for so long the lead was
Too onerous. I fluffed my lines and lacked
Stage presence, ducking into the car without
Taking a final bow the audience didn't expect.

Still the backcloth was good, the small
House and the dog and the rutted lane
Fixed in time, and the old female figure
(Was it the mother?) forever wiping her nose.


## A True Story
(so P.S. tells me)


No blacks, no Irish, no dogs.
I read the rooms to let near
Gloucester Road, brushed my hackles
Flat and continued my search. Then

It wasn't the jibe of race but
The spot between black and dog.
My blood burned and my thick
Tongue filled my gob, blocking the
Words of release, black Irish dog.

I found a room, a den between two
Floors, a curtain to draw behind
And a bed for the neutral night. I
Found love too, more than my ire deserved.
She poured ointment on my tongue. I
Lapped affection, licked kisses on her face.

The dogs were rehabilitated first. The
Blacks legalised on penny postcards on shop
Fronts. I trimmed my words for the Anglo-
Saxon ear. Nothing remains but a green

Passport. Recently on returning from Paris
A customs official, concerned about rabies,
Asked if I were bringing in a dog.

# BIOGRAPHICAL NOTES

WENDY COPE. Born in Erith, Kent, in 1945 and educated at Farringtons School and St Hilda's College, Oxford, where she read history. She teaches in a London primary school. Two of the poems included here were first published in her pamphlet *Across the City* (Priapus Press, 1980); others have previously appeared in *Aquarius, Bananas, New Poetry, New Statesman, PEN Broadsheet, Quarto* and *The Times Literary Supplement*. 'Proverbial Ballade' was broadcast on *Poetry Now* (BBC Radio 3) and a recent Radio 3 programme about Jason Strugnell featured several poems from this selection.

DUNCAN FORBES. Born 1947, he was brought up in Plymouth and read English at Corpus Christi College, Oxford. After a spell as a trade-mark agent in London, he now teaches English in Cheltenham. He won a Gregory Award in 1974 and some of the poems printed here have appeared in one or more of the following: *Critical Quarterly, Encounter, Honest Ulsterman, Mandeville Press Dragoncards, New Poetry 3, 4* and *6* (Arts Council), *New Statesman, The Penguin Book of Light Verse, Quarto, South West Review* and *The Times Literary Supplement*. He is married with a son and a daughter.

MICHAEL HOFMANN. Born in Freiburg in 1957. Came to England aged four and went to schools in Bristol, Edinburgh and Winchester. In between times spent two years in America. Read English at Cambridge and is presently a research student at Trinity College, working on foreign influences on Robert Lowell. Edited an issue of *Granta* on contemporary German and Austrian literature. Started writing four years ago. The poems in this selection first appeared in *London Magazine*, *London Review of Books*, *New Statesman*, *Quarto* and *The Times Literary Supplement*. 'Hausfrauenchor' was a runner-up in the 1980 Arvon Poetry Competition.

MEDBH McGUCKIAN. Born in Belfast in 1950, where she attended a convent school. From 1968 to 1974 she studied English at the Queen's University, Belfast, eventually taking an M.A. degree. She is married to a geography teacher, has one son, and herself lives and teaches in Belfast. She has published in pamphlet form with Ulsterman Publications (*Portrait of Joanna*) and Interim Press (*Single Ladies*). A selection has appeared recently in Blackstaff's *Trio Poetry 2*. Her poems also feature in the new Penguin anthology and a first book is being planned for spring 1982 with O.U.P. 'The Heiress' and 'The Sitting' have been published in the *New Statesman*. In 1979 she won the National Poetry Competition, organised jointly by the Poetry Society and BBC 2, and in 1980 she won a Gregory Award.

BLAKE MORRISON. Born in Skipton, Yorkshire, in 1950, and educated at the universities of Nottingham and London. His critical study *The Movement: English Poetry and Fiction of the 1950s* was published in 1980, he received an E. C. Gregory award in the same year, and he is co-editor (with Andrew Motion) of a new Penguin anthology of contemporary British poetry. He lives in London where he worked for three years as Poetry and Fiction Editor of the *Times Literary Supplement*. He is now Deputy Literary Editor of the *Observer*. Acknowledgments are due to the editors of the *New Statesman*, *Encounter*, *Quarto* and the *London Review of Books*, in whose magazines some of these poems first appeared.

SIMON RAE. Born 1952. He read English and history at Kent University, where he was joint winner of the T. S. Eliot Poetry Prize in 1974. After teaching at Banbury School for two years he became a graduate student at Lincoln College, Oxford. The poems included here have appeared in *Bananas*, *Honest Ulsterman*, *New Statesman*, *New Poetry 4*, *6* and *7* (Arts Council), *Other Poetry*, *Quarto*, *The Times Literary Supplement*. 'The Tools' was read on *Closedown* on BBC 2 in 1978, and 'First Snow' won a second prize in the National Poetry Competition in 1979. He won a Gregory Award in 1980.

JOE SHEERIN. Born in Dargoon, County Leitrim, Southern Ireland, and attended primary school there. Coming to England in the 1950s, he worked, among other jobs, on buildings sites and in factories. After travelling in Europe he entered London University, where he took a degree in German and, later, a degree in English literature. He held a teaching fellowship at McMaster University, Ontario, where he took an M.A. He is married with two children and teaches English at a comprehensive school in Colchester. The poems printed here have appeared in the following: *Best of the Poetry Year 6*, *Helix*, *Hibernian Poetry*, *Honest Ulsterman*, *New Irish Writing* and *New Poetry 4* (Arts Council). 'Rescuing a Princess' was broadcast on *Poetry Now* (BBC Radio 3).